# A Note to Parents and Teachers

*Eyewitness Readers* is a compelling new reading programme for children. *Eyewitness* has become the most trusted name in illustrated books and this new series combines the highly visual *Eyewitness* approach with engaging, easy-to-read stories. Each *Eyewitness Reader* is guaranteed to capture a child's interest while developing his or her reading skills, general knowledge and love of reading.

The books are written by leading children's authors and are designed in conjunction with literacy experts, including Cliff Moon M.Ed., Honorary Fellow of the University of Reading. Cliff Moon spent many years as a teacher and teacher educator specializing in reading. He has written more than 140 books for children and teachers and he reviews regularly for teachers' journals.

The four levels of *Eyewitness Readers* are aimed at different reading abilities, enabling you to choose the books that are exactly right for each child.

**Level One** – Beginning to read
**Level Two** – Beginning to read alone
**Level Three** – Reading alone
**Level Four** – Proficient readers

The "normal" age at which a child begins to read can be anywhere from three to eight years old, so these levels are intended only as a general guideline.

No matter which level you select, you can be sure that you're helping children learn to read, then read to learn!

# A Dorling Kindersley Book

Visit us on the World Wide Web at
http://www.dk.com

**Project Editor** Mary Atkinson
**Art Editor** Susan Calver
**Senior Editor** Linda Esposito
**Deputy Managing Art Editor**
Jane Horne
**Production** Kate Oliver
**Picture Researcher** Jo Carlill
**Illustrator** Norman Young
**Reading Consultant**
Cliff Moon M.Ed.

Published in Great Britain by
Dorling Kindersley Limited
9 Henrietta Street
London WC2E 8PS

2 4 6 8 10 9 7 5 3 1

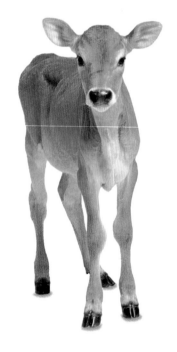

Copyright © 1998 Dorling Kindersley Limited, London
Photography: duckling in water pp10–11 copyright © 1991
Barrie Watts; sheepdog p28 copyright © 1991 Philip Dowell

Eyewitness Readers™ is a trademark of
Dorling Kindersley Ltd.

A CIP catalogue record for this book is
available from the British Library.

ISBN 0-7513-5737-5

Colour reproduction by Colourscan, Singapore
Printed and bound in the U.S.A. by World Color

The publisher would like to thank the following for
their kind permission to reproduce their photographs:
Key: t=top, b=below, l=left, r=right, c=centre
**Bruce Coleman Collection:** 13tr, 13cr, 32clb;
**Holt Studios International:** Primrose Peacock 14bl;
**Telegraph Colour Library:** Thompson Studio Recording 14tl;
**Tony Stone Images:** 10tl.

Additional photography by Peter Anderson, Jon Bouchier,
Jane Burton, Peter Chadwick, Gordon Clayton,
Philip Dowell, Mike Dunning, Andreas Von Einsiedel,
Dave King, Bill Ling, Kim Taylor, and Barrie Watts.

EYEWITNESS ● READERS
Level 1 BEGINNING TO READ

# A Day at
# Greenhill Farm

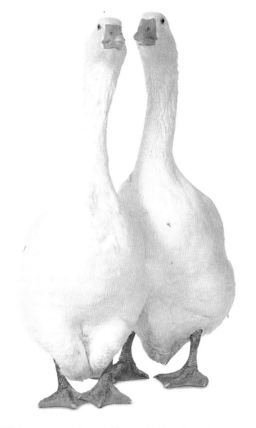

Written by Sue Nicholson

DORLING KINDERSLEY
London • New York • Moscow • Sydney
Visit us on the World Wide Web at http://www.dk.com

It is early in the morning.
The farm is quiet.

Then the cock
begins to crow.

Cock-a-doodle-doo!

What a noise!

He wakes up
all the other
farm animals.

In the barn,
mother hen begins to cluck.
One of her eggs
is ready to hatch.

Cluck
Cluck

Peck, peck, peck!
A tiny chick pecks
through its shell.

Then more eggs crack open and
five cheeping chicks hatch out.

Cheep   Cheep   Cheep   Cheep   Cheep

Some other babies
hatch from eggs too.

Quack
Quack

Mother duck has
six baby ducklings.

Mother goose has
four baby goslings.

Honk
Honk

The ducks waddle
down to the pond
for a morning dip.

Their wide,
webbed feet
push through
the water.

The ducklings have
soft, fluffy feathers
called down.

down

Quack

Soon they will grow
long, oily feathers
to keep them warm and dry.

Mother goose
feels hungry.

So she snaps up
grass and weeds
in her bright orange bill.

bill

Honk

She flaps her wings and honks
if anyone comes near her goslings.

wing

 At milking time
the cows come
to the gate.

The farmer milks the cows.
He will sell the milk
for people to drink.

The cows go back
to their field
to munch grass.

Munch
Munch

Munch
Munch

15

Other animals are hungry too.

A sheep
nibbles hay.

So does a goat.

The pigs
hunt for food
in the barn.

One pig has her snout
in a bucket of corn!

snout

All the farm babies
tell their mothers
they are hungry.

"Baa, baa," says the lamb
to mother sheep.

Baa
Baa

"Naa, naa," says the kid
to mother goat.

Naa
Naa

The piglets squeal and squeak.
Then they drink their mother's milk.

There are even more babies
on the farm.

Meow

The cat has kittens.

The mouse
has baby mice.

Squeak

Squeak

Meow

One day the kittens
will chase the mice!

All the baby animals
love to play.

The kids butt each other
with their horns.

horns

The piglets
roll about
in the mud.

Out in the fields,
the lambs skip and jump.
Skip, hop, jump!
One tiny hoof
follows another.

hoof

One calf has lost his mother.
"Moo! Moo!" he calls.
His mother calls back.
She is not far away.

Moo
Moo

Mother horse has
a baby foal.
He is only
two months old.
But he can run fast.

The foal races
around the field
with his mane
blowing in the wind.

mane

All that running
makes him hungry.
So he eats an apple.

Woof

In the afternoon,
the sheepdog helps
the farmer round up
the sheep.

Then the farmer
shears the sheep.

28

The sheep look smaller and cleaner without their wool.

Baa
Baa

wool

Evening comes. It is dark.
The farm is quiet.

The chicks ...

and the lambs ...

Zzzzzzz

and the piglets fall fast asleep.

But the cat will keep watch
until the cock crows again.

# Farm Vocabulary

down
page 11

horns
page 22

bill
page 12

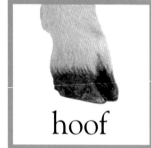
hoof
page 24

wing
page 13

mane
page 26

snout
page 17

wool
page 29